THE UNFOLDING DRAMA
OF THE BIBLE

A HADDAM HOUSE PUBLICATION

NOW REPRINTED AS A REFLECTION BOOK

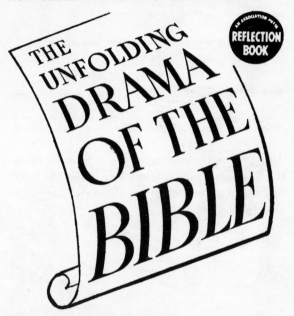

THE UNFOLDING DRAMA OF THE BIBLE

AN ASSOCIATION PRESS
REFLECTION BOOK

EIGHT STUDIES INTRODUCING

THE BIBLE AS A WHOLE

Prepared by BERNHARD W. ANDERSON
Dean, Drew Theological Seminary
Author of REDISCOVERING THE BIBLE

Association Press • New York

NORMA PERKINS HAGAN LIBRARY

THE UNFOLDING DRAMA OF THE BIBLE

————

Copyright © 1957 by
National Board of Young Men's Christian Associations

————

Association Press, 291 Broadway, New York 7, N. Y.

All rights reserved, including the right of reproduction in whole or in part in any form, under the International, Pan-American, and Universal Copyright Conventions.

Library of Congress catalog card number: 57-11608

Printed in the United States of America

Contents

WHAT THEY SAY ABOUT
The Unfolding Drama of the Bible

"This little book is a map showing the main highways through the Bible. It seems incredible that eight short studies can provide an accurate road map of the Bible, but Dr. Anderson succeeds. It is a guide that anyone can use by himself, though mainly it is intended for discussion groups. There are very pertinent and provocative questions appended to each section (some of them with no easy answers) to insure a maximum of individual and group thinking along the way.

"Dr. Anderson's guide provides you with all the information and insight that is essential for the first stages of the most exciting and rewarding journey of the mind (and spirit and heart) you are ever likely to undertake. I recommend it without hesitation."—Dr. Chad Walsh, quoted in *Religious Book Club Bulletin.*

"Dr. Anderson is a breath of fresh air! His eight studies cover the main streams of God's pursuit of man as written down in the Bible. This is a superb 'first step' for all of us to understand where we fit in God's drama of history. Here is a Bible study outline you can't afford to miss!"—from *Memo to Staff*, issued by Leadership Services, National Board, YWCA.

The Unfolding Drama of the Bible unfolds in amazingly brief compass the main theme of the Bible. The central problem is posed in picturesque story form in the opening chapters of Genesis. It is seen as man's separation from God, from his fellow men and within himself. In other words, man has cut himself off from the deep resources of creativity and fullness of life which are his birthright. The drama is the story of the consequences of this separation and of God's actions to overcome this separation as seen in the thousand-year span of history the

Bible covers. God's purpose is revealed in this history—and in ours.

"Brief enough even for busy people, these studies comprehend the full sweep of history. An eye-opening introduction to those who have no acquaintance with the Bible, they reveal new depths of understanding to those familiar with the Bible."—Edward L. Nestingen, Program Secretary, National Student YMCA.

"This masterful condensation of the biblical revelation achieves the author's purpose to introduce the Bible as a whole and to urge the importance of reading it not as a textbook but as 'a letter from God with your personal address on it.' "—*The Pulpit.*

Introducing
the Bible Study

A New Horizon

In one of his well-known sonnets John Keats tells how in reading Chapman's translation of Homer he experienced the elation of a new discovery.

> Then felt I like some watcher of the skies
> When a new planet swims into his ken;
> Or, like stout Cortez, when with eagle eyes
> He stared at the Pacific—and all his men
> Looked at each other with a wild surmise—
> Silent, upon a peak in Darien.

In our day many have had a similar experience in reading the Bible. Bible Study, of the kind you are about to engage in, can have the result of opening your eyes to an entirely new vista, of giving you a new perspective upon the meaning of your life and the whole historical drama.

There are two ways to study the Bible. The

first way is appropriate to classroom or academic study. Using this approach, one *looks at* the Bible from the outside as a spectator. He learns many interesting facts about the Bible such as the literary process which brought it to final shape, or the cultural and historical background of the various books. He is curious about the ideas of the Bible, and perhaps he masters these ideas well enough to pass a course examination with flying colors. This approach has its place, but it is not the one we shall assume in these studies. The second approach is one in which together we shall attempt to *stand within* the Bible and to look out at the world through the window of biblical faith. We shall read the Bible with personal concern, realizing that it is not a textbook but "a letter from God with your personal address on it," as Kierkegaard once said. We shall listen to the word which is spoken to each of us through the medium of the sacred page.

God's Manifesto

The uniqueness of this Bible Study arises from the uniqueness of the Bible itself. It is the Christian claim that the perspective which is set forth in the Bible has been provided by God through his own self-revelation. This is what puts the Bible in a class all by itself. Christians affirm that the Bible *contains* the Word of God. Just as in our everyday experience a "word" is a bridge of communication between persons, so likewise God's Word is the medium of his communication to man. This does not mean that the Bible contains the literal words of God, taken down by human stenographers. Many people have been unnecessarily alienated from the Bible by the claims of "fundamentalists" who, with more enthusiasm than wisdom, have insisted that the words of the Bible have the same infallibility as Roman Catholics claim for the *ex cathedra* pronouncements of the Pope. No, the Bible does not record divine dictation. Rather, within the Bible is disclosed the meaning of personal life and history. And according to the testimony of faith this disclosure of meaning is God's Word, God's revelation. Together we shall look beyond the surface of the words for this meaning.[1]

The Bible may be described as "God's Manifesto." The dictionary defines a manifesto as "a public declaration, usually of a sovereign or political group, showing intentions and motives." So, for instance, the Communist Manifesto is a declaration of the alleged meaning of the economic crisis and the direction of the historical process; and to be a Communist is to see things from this perspective. In a more special sense the Bible is, for the Christian, God's Manifesto. God is the Sovereign who declares the inner meaning of a historical crisis and discloses the direction of the whole human drama. His revelation is given in the events of which the Bible is the record and the witness, events which come to climax and fulfillment in Jesus Christ. And to be a Christian is to see everything from this perspective.

Now this does not mean that one has to be a convinced Christian before he can get anything out of the Bible. As Paul Lehmann says, "The Bible has a curious slant in favor of the unbeliever; the unbeliever, that is, who is really honest about his unbelief, and really curious about the full diversity and complexity of the world in which he lives."[2] The only condition for fruitful Bible Study is that you come with an infinite concern about the question: "What is the meaning of *my* life and the historical crisis in which I and my community are involved?" Instead of saying with Henry Ford that "history is bunk," you must be willing to let the past—this biblical past—speak to you and become real in the present. You must meet others in the group as persons, respecting their individuality and being willing to learn from the conversation. You must come with the intention of wrestling seriously and honestly with the meaning of a biblical passage—not to air your private opinions or prejudices. You must expect to be questioned by the Bible, even as you bring your own questions to the Bible. It may be that in this give-and-take experience you will discover an entirely new dimension of life.

The Bible as a Drama

In the following studies we shall tackle the whole Bible. This may seem as foolish as American tourists who breeze through the Louvre museum in Paris as though they were trying to establish a new track record. We shall admit at the outset that this approach runs the risk of superficiality. It is to be hoped that you will have time enough to stake your claims so that later you can come back to sink your shafts more deeply. However, most of us lack any sense of the Bible as a whole. We know a few snatches of Scripture here and there, like the twenty-third Psalm or the Sermon on the Mount, but are very hazy—if not completely ignorant—about the larger context within which these favorite passages have meaning. We need to stand back from the trees so that we may see the woods. This is the justification for this study of the Bible in eight units.

In these studies we shall think of the Bible as presenting a historical drama. To be sure, this figure of speech is not found anywhere in the Bible itself, but it is a convenient and appropriate way of viewing the Bible as a whole. Several characteristics of a drama spring to mind immediately. For one thing, a drama has a beginning and an end; it starts somewhere and goes somewhere. Also, it has a cast of persons and the story deals with their hopes and fears, laughter and sorrow, ambitions and tragedy. Further, a drama has a plot which moves forward through the various acts toward a denouement when the episodes which took place at the beginning are understood in their larger meaning. In a drama there is a great deal of diversity: different personalities, different attitudes expressed, different episodes which take place at different times and in different settings. But underlying all this variety is the movement of the plot toward its resolution.

The Bible, too, has a unity which is like that of a drama. It moves from beginning to end, from Creation to New Creation. The story deals with men's hopes and fears, their joys and sorrows, their ambitions and tragedy. There is a great deal of diversity in the Bible: different authors, different historical situations, different kinds of theological expression; but underlying all this great variety is the dramatic movement which binds the whole together. However, this drama is unique in that God appears in the cast. He is not only behind the scenes prompting and directing the drama, but he enters onto the stage of history as the Chief Actor—the protagonist. The plot is the working out of God's purpose in spite of all efforts to oppose it. The denouement is reached when the Crucifixion-Resurrection is proclaimed as the sign of his victory, and in the light of this climactic event the earlier stages of the story are understood with deeper meaning.

A Drama in Three Acts

Using this dramatic scheme, the eight studies in this series may be outlined as follows:

Prologue: In the Beginning (Study I)

Act I

    Scene 1:   Encounter with God (Study II)

    Scene 2:   The Discipline of Disaster (Study III)

Act II

    Scene 1:   The Second Exodus (Study IV)

    Scene 2:   The People of the Law (Study V)

Act III

    Scene 1:   Victory Through Defeat (Study VI)

    Scene 2:   The Church and the World (Study VII)

Epilogue: History's Finale (Study VIII)

In the course of the studies it will become clear that each of the acts deals with a decisive historical event which is viewed as a "mighty act" of God. These three events are: the exodus of the Israelites from Egypt, the exile of conquered Israelites into Babylonia and their providential return to their homeland, and the crucifixion and resurrection of Jesus. The selection of passages for study has to be somewhat arbitrary, for obviously we can deal with only a small fraction of the Bible.[3] Our purpose is not to make an exhaustive study of the Bible, but to enter into the inner meaning of these three crucial events in the biblical drama.

One concluding word: don't suppose that this is the kind of drama we can view from a grandstand seat. We are not to be spectators of something that happened once upon a time. If this Bible Study is to be taken seriously, we must be willing to get onto the biblical stage and participate personally in the dramatic movement—act by act. Perhaps this warning is unnecessary, for it is the testimony of experience that as men read the Bible the Holy Spirit convinces them that God speaks to the reader personally and makes him an actor in the drama. Paul Minear has put the matter this way:

It is as if in the theater, where I am hugely enjoying an esthetic view of life, God interrupts the show with a stentorian announcement: "Is John Smith in the house?" And I am John Smith. And the interruption continues: "Report immediately . . . for a task intended for you alone!"[4]

So, realizing that God is apt to stop the show and put us into the act, let's begin our study.

Footnotes

1. See B. W. Anderson, *Rediscovering the Bible* (Haddam House: Association Press, 1951), Ch. 1. Hereafter this book will be referred to as RB.

2. Paul Lehmann, *The Death of Jesus Christ*, A Bible Study on What Led Christians to Study the Bible (USCC, 1951).

3. Usually two or three biblical passages are chosen for each study unit. If only one session is devoted to each unit, the leader must determine

which passage is to be the focus of discussion in the study group. Otherwise the group may want to stay with a given unit for more than one session.

4. Paul S. Minear, *Eyes of Faith* (Westminster Press, 1946), p. 19.

In the Beginning

One of the daringly original convictions of the Bible is summed up in the words of an ancient creed: "I believe in God the Father Almighty, Maker of heaven and earth." We are so used to speaking of God as Creator that we scarcely realize the revolutionary implications of this belief. According to the religions of ancient Egypt and Babylonia the gods were in nature, for nature with its creative powers was regarded as being a manifestation of the divine. Likewise for the ancient Greeks the gods were immanent or

---

STUDY PASSAGES

1. Genesis 1:1 to 2:3 (see Psalm 8)
2. Genesis 2:4 (beginning with second half of verse) to 3:24

"inside" nature, and since the world was regarded as being eternal there was no room in their thought for Creation. The Bible stands in flat contradiction to these views. God is not in nature; he is not a natural process. Rather, God is "over against" nature, and nature displays the handiwork of her Creator.

Life's Deepest Dimension

A road block which stands in the way of our approach to Genesis 1—3 is our slavery to the scientific attitude. Too many people try to modernize these chapters into a scientific account, and to harmonize the narrative with modern scientific theories. Some have argued, for instance, that the "days" mentioned in Genesis 1 correspond to geological periods, or that the doctrine of evolution is implicit in the whole account. But this is to miss the whole point of the biblical narrative. The central issue here is that of the *meaning* of man's life in the natural world, and this is not a scientific question, properly speaking. The Bible asks—and answers—the "ultimate question": What is the origin, meaning, and destiny of man's life? You must be on guard against reading into the biblical narrative the presuppositions of our scientific age.

If you have had a course in the Old Testament you probably know that actually we have two narratives of the Creation, the first running from Genesis 1:1 to the end of Genesis 2:3, and the second beginning with the last half of Genesis 2:4. The first of these narratives was written in the period which we are symbolizing as Act II (about 550 B.C.), and the second comes from the period of Act I (perhaps as early as 950 B.C.—during the era of Solomon). Therefore both stories really reflect the meaning of these acts of the biblical drama, just as they reflect the language and culture of their period. (See RB, pp. 43-52.) The important thing to notice, however, is that both stories affirm that the meaning of human life is not disclosed in nature, but in relationship to God who transcends the natural world. To use modern words, God is the Ground of all that is. These stories are really "word pictures" which portray life's deepest dimension.[1]

It would be helpful if we had in the English language two words which corresponded to German *Weltbild* (world picture) and *Weltanschauung* (world perspective). The "world picture" of Genesis 1 is the naïve one of antiquity: a picture of the earth as a flat surface, resting on the primeval "waters beneath the earth" and separated from "the waters above the earth" by a blue firmament. The "world perspective," however, concerns the meaning of man's life on the natural stage. Man is able to survey and control nature, to search for the good, the true, and the beautiful, to remember the past, to hope for the future, and to decide in the present. This is the divine endowment which elevates man above the animals and gives him the status of a creature who is "a little lower than

God" (Psalm 8), or "made in the image of God." The story in Genesis 2 is written from a similar perspective: like the animals, man is made from the dust and returns to the dust, but his ability to name the animals indicates his dominion over the animal kingdom (2:19-20). Today we know about the chemical constituents of this "dust," and we have a much more adequate "world picture"; but have we gone beyond the biblical perspective on the meaning of man's life in the natural world? (See RB, pp. 237-248).

Herbert Butterfield, professor of modern history in the University of Cambridge, has written some words which are relevant to the Creation story:

The historian does not treat man as the student of biology seems to—does not regard him as essentially a part of nature or consider him primarily in this aspect. He picks up the other end of the stick and envisages a world of human relations standing, so to speak, over against nature—he studies that new kind of life which man has superimposed on the jungle, the forest and the waste. Since this world of

human relations is the historian's universe, we may
say that history is a human drama, a drama of personalities, taking place as it were, on the stage of
nature, and amid its imposing scenery.[2]

Thus we speak of the "human drama," al-
though often in purely humanistic terms. The
Creation story underscores the conviction
that the drama is not just about man, for it
has its beginning and end in the purpose of
God. History is *His*-Story.

Paradise Lost

Probably you should devote most of your
attention to the narrative of "Paradise Lost"
in Genesis 2 and 3, for in this story are to be
found the profoundest insights into the human problem. Don't be disturbed by the
picturesque and naïve form of the language,
as though this marked the story as inferior
to that of Genesis 1. These chapters focus
upon God's *personal* relation to man, and we
have no other language to portray this relationship except the rich symbols of human

language. You should reflect on the meaning of some of these symbols: the Tree of Life, Adam's rib, the serpent, the forbidden fruit, nakedness, and so forth. Read the story with poetic imagination.

This is not just a story of something that happened once upon a time, but is a profound description of any human life. Indeed, the word Adam in Hebrew really is a generic term for "man, mankind." Adam represents Everyman. Surely there is in human experience a melancholy awareness that man's life is not what it ought to be, that somehow or somewhere he has lost the peace and wholeness for which his existence was intended. Conflict, anxiety, insecurity, exploitation, suffering—these are not intended to be "normal," even though they are life's daily realities. Why is this? Unlike Marxism, which traces the problem to economic factors, and looks back to a primitive classless society, the Bible traces the problem to man's estrangement from God, to man's *will*. (See RB, pp. 248-254.)

Notice that the Adam story falls into three episodes:

a) In the first episode Adam is the *gardener*. He has a God-given *task*: to dress and keep the garden in faithfulness to his Creator. Work, when performed in trust and responsibility, is man's God-given dignity.

b) In the second episode Adam is the *rebel*. His freedom makes it possible for him to obey or to disobey God's sovereign will, and he cannot resist the tempting possibilities of life on his own terms. The phrase "knowing good and evil" is a Hebrew expression for coming to maturity, as when a child leaves the age of innocence and attains the age of discretion. So sin is "growing up to the stature of manhood in man's own way" (A. G. Hebert); it is man's declaration of independence from God. Above all, we must understand that sin is not just a matter of doing something immoral, of being "bad boys." Sin is alienation from God, from one's fellow men, and from one's truest self

—an alienation which is rooted in a rebellious will. Sin is man's false maturity.[3]

c) In the third episode Adam is the *fugitive*—cast out from the primeval peace of the garden into a restless life of insecurity and conflict. The rest of the Bible is a commentary on this truth, that when men are estranged from God they are separated from their fellow men and from their deepest selves. For man belongs to God by nature, and cannot find peace outside the relationship of dependence for which he was created. So Augustine began his *Confessions* with this prayer: "O Lord, thou hast made us for thyself, and our hearts are restless until they rest in thee."

Questions to Think About

1. What is the religious meaning of the doctrine that God is the Creator? Why is this "truth" of a different order than what we usually regard as "scientific truth"?

2. What is meant in Genesis 1 when it is

said that man is made in "the image of God"? Does the story in Genesis 2–3 cast any light on this?

3. Do you see any connection between Adam's awareness of the threat of death and the misuse of his God-given freedom? In other words, is the occasion for "sin" anxiety about our insecurity within nature? See William Spurrier, *Guide to the Christian Faith* (Scribner, 1952), pp. 64-69.

4. "Sin is man's false maturity." What does this mean? Can sin find expression in moral goodness as well as in immoral acts? See RB, pp. 66-71.

5. What is wrong with the Marxist view that the troubles of history can be traced to economic factors, and that when these are changed human nature will be transformed and men will live in the peace of utopia? Is the biblical portrait of the human situation more realistic?

6. What is the meaning of "original sin"?

James Bryce observed that our American Constitution was written by men who believed in original sin. Is this reflected in the constitutional restraint on the exercise of power?

7. What does it mean to take the Bible seriously rather than literally? Does the Bible give scientific information which could be acquired otherwise through experimental research?

Footnotes

1. See Reinhold Niebuhr, "As Deceivers, Yet True," in *Beyond Tragedy* (Charles Scribner's Sons, 1938), Ch. 1.

2. Herbert Butterfield, *Christianity and History* (Charles Scribner's Sons, 1950), pp. 6-7. Used by permission.

3. See Paul Tillich's sermon, "You Are Accepted," in *The Shaking of the Foundations* (Charles Scribner's Sons, 1948), Ch. 19.

STUDY II:

Encounter with God

With the Exodus or the "going out" of the Israelites from Egypt, the curtain rises on the first major event of the biblical drama. Every historical community looks back to some decisive event as its birth hour. Of this event the members of the community can say: "This is what brought us forth upon the stage of history as a people of destiny. This is where the meaning of our history was disclosed." In this country, for instance, we look back to the time of the Revolutionary

---

STUDY PASSAGES
1. Exodus 3:1-21
2. Exodus 20:1-17
3. Exodus 24:3-8
4. Deuteronomy 4:25-40 and 8:1-18

War. It is significant that in a grave crisis Abraham Lincoln turned back to that creative year of 1776. "Four score and seven years ago our fathers brought forth upon this continent a new nation, conceived in liberty. . . ."

Israel's Birth Hour

It was similar in the case of the community known as Israel. However, the analogy of America and Israel breaks down at this point: for Israel the Exodus was not just a creative event; it was an event of revelation. It was a time of encounter with the Lord of history. Israel's ancient confession of faith ran something like this: "Our forefathers were pilgrims in Palestine. A small band went down to Egypt in a time of famine, and when Israel multiplied, the Egyptian king subjected us to slave labor on public works. But the Lord, the God of our fathers, saw our affliction and heard our cry. With many miraculous signs of his presence in our midst he delivered us from the Pharaoh's yoke, and brought us into a new land where we could find our freedom in serving him." (A paraphrase of Deuteronomy 26:5-10.)

The best way to prepare for this study is to read as much as possible of Exodus 1—24 and the commentary on the meaning of these events found in Deuteronomy 1—11. Remember that our primary concern is not with critical details. We want to enter into the inner meaning of the event of the Exodus—the meaning which was kept alive and relived in every annual celebration of the Passover feast. This can be done by concentrating on the passages that have been selected, with perhaps side reference to Deuteronomy 4:25-40 or 8:1-18. It would be advisable to bypass the question of particular miracle stories until you have come to terms with the central historical miracle: the Exodus. (See RB, Ch. 3.)

God Introduces Himself

A good place to begin the discussion is the story of Moses' call in Exodus 3, for this narrative introduces the theme of the whole book of Exodus. Rather than tripping over details, read the passage with religious imagination. Perhaps you will find that the dialogue corresponds to your own deepest experience. Notice that Moses was addressed by God not as he was overwhelmed with the grandeur of nature, but as he was brooding over the meaning of what was happening in history. Observe the emphasis upon God's entrance into the historical struggle: "I have seen the plight of my people," "I have heard their cry," "I know their sorrows," "I have come down to rescue them."

The story of Moses' encounter with God is paralleled in other accounts, like the story of Elijah at Mt. Horeb (Sinai) (I Kings 19), the call of a prophet (see Isaiah 6; Amos 7:10-17), the psalmist's awareness of the inescapable God (Psalm 139), or the symphony of voices in the New Testament which affirm that God has spoken to men through Jesus Christ. Therefore, when we speak of "revelation" we are referring to a personal encounter in which God makes *himself* known. God introduces himself, so to speak; he makes himself known through his word and his action. Perhaps a human analogy will help to clarify this. We cannot really know any person unless he reveals himself to us through his speech and actions. We can know a lot of things *about* John Jones—his family background, his education, his job, his physical appearance, and so forth; but we cannot really know John Jones *himself* unless he chooses to disclose his inner self through what he says and does. So it is with God. We cannot know God himself unless he chooses to reveal himself in prophetic word and divine action. Revelation is not receiving ideas about God, but is rather to meet God, to be introduced to God personally. And the meeting place is the concrete life-situations of history.[1]

The Covenant Faith

The next two passages (20:1-17 and 24:3-8) should be considered together, for they deal with Israel's response to God's intervention on her behalf. Here we come upon the central motif of Israel's faith: the Covenant. (Old Testament really means "Old Covenant.") As in the case of the "marriage covenant" this biblical covenant is a personal relationship based on commitment and trust. However, unlike the marriage covenant it is more unilateral in character, for it is a covenant between unequals (God and man). It is God who "makes" or "gives" the Covenant, and Israel responds in gratitude, reverence, and loyalty. (See RB, Ch. 4.)

The following points deserve your attention:

a) God takes the initiative in establishing this relationship. He steps onto the stage of history and confronts men with his sovereign claim. Israel did not choose, but was *chosen*.

Therefore, faith is *wholehearted* response to God's initiative as manifested in his "mighty act" of deliverance.

b) This relationship places men under an unconditional demand: "Thou shalt." God addresses men in categorical terms, and men are responsible to him. One cannot serve God with half a heart, and some other loyalty with the other half of his devotion. Like any absolute commitment, the covenant allegiance is essentially a "jealous" one.

c) Faith involves not only obligations toward God, but obligations toward the other members of the covenant community. This is the meaning of the giving of the Law in connection with the making of the Covenant. These laws were often adapted to new cultural circumstances, but the basic principle remained constant: men are absolutely responsible to one another because they are absolutely responsible to God.

d) Ethical responsibility is motivated by gratitude for *what God has done,* that is, his self-revelation in the event of the Exodus. Notice the preface to the Ten Commandments: "I am the Lord your God, who brought you out of the land of Egypt, out of the house of bondage." Men are to obey God, not as slaves driven to their duties, but as sons who have been graciously redeemed.

Chosen for Service

It is important to see how the Exodus story ties up with the dramatic theme of the Book of Genesis. As we saw in the last study, Genesis 1—3 gives a word-picture of the fundamental human situation: man's estrangement from God. We are told in Genesis 12:1-4 that God, to meet this universal human predicament, took appropriate action by calling a man, Abraham, and promising him that his people would be a blessing to the whole earth. The God who speaks to Moses is "the God of the fathers—Abraham, Isaac, and Jacob." Thus the deliverance of the Israelites from Egyptian bondage is viewed in the perspective of God's redemptive concern for all mankind.

Questions to Think About

1. Many philosophers, ancient and modern, have insisted that Reality is to be found "above" history in unchanging Ideas, and religions like Hinduism and Buddhism seek the Divine above the cycle of change and growth. Do you see the radical difference between these views and the biblical perspective?

2. What does it mean to say that "God acts in history"? (See RB, Ch. 2.) Is that a realistic way to view the present world crisis? Does Exodus 3:7-8 describe God's attitude toward suppressed races and nations today?

3. In his book, *I and Thou* (p. 45), the Jewish philosopher Martin Buber writes: "The true community does not arise through people's having feelings for one another

(though indeed not without it), but through, first, their taking their stand in living mutual relation with the living Centre, and second, their being in living mutual relation with one another." Is this the meaning of the Covenant?

4. A justice of the Supreme Court recently defended a decision by pointing out that in modern society "there are no absolutes." How does this square with the covenant faith? Would you say that the Ten Commandments are absolutely binding in every situation?

5. "Thou shalt have no other gods before me." What are some of the "gods" that men worship today? What does God's jealousy mean in our situation?

6. When does God speak most authentically: when we are enjoying the beauties of nature, or when we are sensitive to the meaning of our historical crisis and alert to our responsibilities as citizens?

7. Religion is often defined as man's search for God. Does this do justice to the biblical faith?

Footnote

1. See Paul S. Minear, *Eyes of Faith* (Westminster Press, 1946), Ch. 1; Martin Buber, *I and Thou* (Edinburgh: T. & T. Clark, 1937); Martin Buber, *Eclipse of God* (Harper & Brothers, 1952), Ch. 3.

STUDY III:

The Discipline of Disaster

This is a study in tragedy. During Jeremiah's long career as a prophet in Jerusalem (626-587 B.C.), events move swiftly and inexorably toward the precipice of national disaster. The very foundations shake under the shattering impact of historical events. And finally the curtain of the first main act of the biblical drama comes down on a scene of utter ruin: the Temple is destroyed, the nation has fallen, and the cream of the popu-

---

STUDY PASSAGES
1. Jeremiah 1:4-10
2. Jeremiah 2:1-13
3. Jeremiah 7:1-15
4. Jeremiah 31:31-34

---

lation has been carried away into foreign exile.

The People That Walked in Darkness

To appreciate the full pathos of the tragedy let us telescope Israel's history, from the period of the Exodus to the fall of the nation, into a short summary. After the miraculous deliverance from Egypt the Israelites were forged together into a community in the experiences of the desert. With a sense of God-given destiny, they moved into the Land of Promise, where, under the leadership of Joshua and his successors, they successfully maintained a foothold despite enemy pressures. In time the community became a nation, and under the leadership of David rose to a height of prestige and glory. But during the oppressive reign of his son, Solomon, there was great restiveness beneath the surface of the nation's glory, and at his death the volcano of revolution broke loose. The once united kingdom was split into North and South by civil strife. Not only were these kingdoms involved in fratricidal rivalry and warfare, but in time they were drawn into the power struggle of the ancient Near East. Crushed beneath the heel of the conqueror, the Northern Kingdom was destroyed by the Assyrians in 722 B.C., and the Southern Kingdom was finished off by the Babylonians in the fateful year 587 B.C.

During this tumultuous period there appeared a remarkable succession of prophets —men like Samuel, Elijah, Amos, Hosea, Isaiah, Jeremiah, and Ezekiel. In all ancient history there was nothing which matched Israelite prophecy. Many people today suppose that a prophet is a kind of palm reader who says, "Let me tell you your future." This is a caricature of prophecy. The true prophet was one who proclaimed the meaning of the historical crisis in the light of Israel's covenant loyalty. He spoke to the urgent and imperative present, by recalling the people to the meaning which had been revealed in the event of the Exodus, and by warning them of the consequences of their actions in the future. As Francis of Sales has pointed out, the tense that matters most in religion is the present. If a biblical prophet speaks to us today, it is because in our time of crisis the present is qualitatively the same, even though the date is in the twentieth century. (See RB, Ch. 5.)

Prophetic Realism

For this study we have arbitrarily selected Jeremiah as representative of the prophetic movement, and a few passages from the Book of Jeremiah as representative of Jeremiah's message. During his lifetime Jeremiah saw the colossal Assyrian empire disintegrate; he witnessed the intense nationalism of the Southern Kingdom, fanned by the hope of independence; he saw the Babylonian empire rise from the ashes of Assyria and spread destruction throughout Palestine. What was the meaning of these events? Like prophets who preceded him, Jeremiah insisted that disaster was a form of discipline, that is, God was *teaching* his people through these tragic events (as the word "discipline" literally suggests). God was actively confronting his people on the plane of history. Therefore, even though there was tragedy, it was *meaningful* tragedy.

The selected passages form a good sequence for discussion. The first one (1:4-10) describes Jeremiah's call in a dialogue which reminds us of the account of Moses' encounter with God. Verse 10 is important. Notice that the first effect of God's Word is destructive; it "roots up and pulls down." Only after this negative or critical function has been performed does it "build and plant." This calls our attention to a characteristic emphasis of the prophetic message: to know God, or rather to be known by him, is to be exposed to his judgment. God sets his plumb line against the unjust structures of society (Amos 7:7-9) and searches the inmost motives of the heart (Psalm 139:1-6). There is no dark corner where the spotlight of his criticism does not reach.

The second passage (2:1-13) reviews the history of Israel in the light of the covenant loyalty. Viewed from this standpoint it is a long history of ingratitude and unfaithfulness to the God who had graciously delivered his people from bondage and brought them into a good land. Men had preferred to live on their own terms, following the idols of their own making. The indictment comes to a resounding climax in verse 13 where the prophet accuses the people of rejecting Him who is the "fountain of living waters" to hew out for themselves "broken cisterns" which can hold no water. This is really the theme which we have encountered previously in the Adam story.

The third passage (7:1-15) comes down to cases more specifically. Here is a bold criticism of religion, that is, the kind of religion which is the tool of the *status quo*. The

prophet warns the people against supposing
that they are "safe" if they go to church,
while their society violates the dignity of
persons and shouts defiance at the sovereignty of God. The ancient shrine at Shiloh
had been destroyed without trace by the
ancient Philistines; and the same would happen to the proud Temple of Jerusalem. For
God is the critic, not the defender, of the historical order. He enters into controversy with
his people.

Judgment in History

Jeremiah's message, then, was that God was
acting in that historical crisis and using the
agency of the Babylonian invader to accomplish his purpose of judgment and discipline.
Men are free to choose their actions, but not
free to escape the consequences of those decisions as long as God is the chief Actor in
history. He acts to overthrow systems of
exploitation, to humble the proud and exalt
those of low degree, and to shatter all false

idols in which men place their trust.[1] But the end of this "shock treatment" is that men may be brought to their senses, and at last find their true community in a New Covenant with God. This is the theme of the final passage (31:31-34), from which the New Testament takes its name.

Questions to Think About

1. Marx observed that the beginning of all criticism is the criticism of religion. In his own way Jeremiah would have agreed. Why?

2. Make a list of some of the "broken cisterns" in which modern men have placed their trust. Would you include education, science, psychology, progress, Communism, "the American Way," organized religion?

3. In his Second Inaugural, Abraham Lincoln said: "If God will that it [the Civil War] continue until every drop of blood drawn by the taskmaster's lash shall be

repaid with two drawn by the sword . . .,
then . . . 'the judgments of the Lord are
true and righteous altogether.' " Does our
present historical crisis disclose the judgment of God? How should this view affect our attitude as American citizens?

4. What is wrong with the view of those
   people who say that religion belongs in
   one sphere and political and economic
   issues in another? Would Jeremiah have
   agreed with the policy of "keeping social
   issues out of the pulpit"?

5. Suppose that Western Civilization should
   fall, as the Roman Empire collapsed in
   the time of Augustine. How would a
   biblical prophet interpret this disaster?

6. What is the meaning of "repentance" or
   turning to God? If America were to repent, would we escape the consequences
   of decisions we have made and actions
   that have already been committed?

7. Jeremiah believed that God was working
   through an unbeliever, Nebuchadnezzar,

to accomplish his purpose in history. What do you think Jeremiah's attitude would be today toward the atheistic rulers of the Kremlin?

Footnote

1. See Herbert Butterfield, *Christianity and History* (Charles Scribner's Sons, 1950), Ch. 3. In this chapter the Cambridge historian affirms that there *is* a discernible element of judgment in history.

STUDY IV:

The Second Exodus

We now come to the second main phase of the biblical drama. The scene opens in Babylonia, to which country Jewish people had been taken after the national debacle of the year 587 B.C. Many of these displaced persons had settled down in relative prosperity and security in the foreign land, but the vision of Jerusalem, destroyed and impoverished, could not be erased from their memories (see Psalm 137). To them the terrible thing was not the physical deprivation but the religious despair and disillusionment which the fall of

---

STUDY PASSAGES

1. Isaiah 40:1-11
2. Isaiah 43:1-21
3. Isaiah 52:13 to 53:12

NORMA PERKINS HAGAN LIBRARY

the nation had occasioned. Jerusalem was more than a city; it was a center of meaning —meaning which had been revealed by God when he delivered Israel from Egypt and providentially guided the course of her history in Palestine.

A Spiritual Blackout

Therefore, the fall of Jerusalem was a spiritual blackout, especially for those who had identified God's purpose in history with the preservation of the nation. See Jeremiah 28 for a vivid description of the tension between nationalism and faith, between popular prophecy and true prophecy. The popular prophet had argued: God is with us in our history, therefore no evil can come upon us. The true prophet had said: God is with us, therefore all securities—Jerusalem, the Temple, religion, the nation—stand under his judgment. It is easy to see how those who had been beguiled by popular prophecy would conclude that

"God had let them down" when Jerusalem was destroyed.

However, the God who performed the miracle of the Exodus was about to make himself known in another "mighty act" of deliverance. This is the testimony of a series of magnificent poems found in the latter part of the Book of Isaiah (chapters 40—55). Speaking to despairing exiles, this prophet announces "good news" that God, who controls the destinies of all nations will make possible the return of Israelites to their homeland where they may take their part in the fulfillment of the divine plan for history. Strikingly, this prophet resorts to the imagery of the exodus from Egypt to describe this new miracle of the "going out" of Israel from Babylonian captivity (44:27; 43:16 f.; 51:10 f.; and compare Exodus 14:15-31). We are justified, therefore, in speaking of this event as "the Second Exodus."

God Is Running History

It is generally recognized that the last part of the present Book of Isaiah, particularly chapters 40 to 55, come from the pen of an unknown prophet who lived during the period of the Exile.[1] In his time the Babylonian empire was declining, and the new factor in the international picture was the rise of a ruler named Cyrus. Having established his control of the Medes and Persians (about 550 B.C.), he pointed his attack at the heart of the Babylonian empire and in 538 B.C. Babylon fell. "Second Isaiah" was active in the period between the rise of the new conqueror and the final capitulation of Babylon, that is, between 550 and 538 B.C. An enlightened monarch, Cyrus policy was that of granting captive peoples the right to live in their own country and to carry on their own traditions. Small wonder that many people, who groaned under the heavy yoke of Babylon, looked to him as a liberator! This is the life-situation to which the Unknown Prophet spoke. His task as a prophet was not just to predict the downfall of Babylon, but to interpret the religious meaning of what was happening. (See RB, pp. 122-133.)

The best way to prepare for this study is to read through all fifteen chapters of Second Isaiah, preferably in the Revised Standard Version. Even from a purely literary point of view this is poetry at its best; and from the perspective of Israel's faith these poems represent the very crown of the Old Testament. The three selected passages set forth the themes which are elaborated with symphonic splendor in the whole work. Remember that our fundamental purpose is to deal with the religious meaning of a crucial event in Israel's history: the return of exiles to Palestine. Above all we must see that the underlying conviction is that world events do not happen by accident, but are subject to the ruling and overruling sovereignty of God, the Creator and Redeemer.[2]

A Herald of Good News

Like a prologue, the first passage (40:1-11) sets the tone of the whole work. The message is a proclamation, the clarion call of a herald. One of the key words in this section is "good news" (verse 9; cf. 52:7), the very word which reappears in our New Testament as "gospel." What is the content of this Good News? It is this: God is about to act, just as at the beginning of Israel's history he had taken the initiative in delivering his people from Egyptian bondage. To an unbeliever, perhaps, there would be nothing extraordinary in the return of Jewish exiles to their homeland; but to those who saw in faith this would be a demonstration of the glory of God. "See, the Lord God is coming with might." Therefore, men were standing on the threshold of the New Age, the Kingdom of God. It is significant that at the beginning of the third stage of the biblical drama John the Baptist recapitulates the theme of this chapter (compare 40:3 with Mark 1:3).

The second passage (43:1-21) is a magnificent statement of the *purposiveness* of history, and Israel's indispensable place in God's plan for all mankind. You should keep in mind that the specific political event in the prophet's mind is the rise to power of Cyrus, the Persian monarch who in another passage is hailed as the agent of the Lord's purpose (see 44:24—45:7). Previous prophets like Isaiah or Jeremiah had insisted that foreign dictators were used by God to accomplish his judgment upon a rebellious people; now this prophet affirms that a foreign conqueror is to be the agent of God's deliverance of these same rebellious people who had already passed through the fires of judgment (see 43:18-25). Not that the people have changed for the better; but only that the undeserved love of God might be made known in its overwhelming glory!

In the present passage notice these two things. (1) Twice the prophet resorts to the image of the Exodus, that is, the passing through the waters of the Red Sea, to describe the new deliverance which is about to take place (verses 2, 16, 17). But this is not just a repetition of the Exodus of old, for historical events are new, unique, and unrepeatable. "Behold I am doing a new thing" (verse 19). (2) The idols of the nations prove their emptiness because of their inability to foretell and control the course of history. To Israel's God this new event is not an accident, but is a part of the working out of his plan in history. Therefore, the event could be "foretold" by prophets (verses 8-13).

The Servant of the Lord

According to Second Isaiah's message, Israel is the Lord's "Servant" (41:8-10; 43:8-13; 44:1-2). This Servant is blind, deaf, and stubborn; nevertheless, despite all his weaknesses, he has been chosen for a unique purpose in history. God had an ulterior motive in delivering Israel from Babylonian bondage, namely, that in this way Israel might be a "light to

the Gentiles" and the witness of God's glory
to the whole world (see 42:1-9).

This theme is developed most profoundly
in our third passage (52:13—53:12), one of
the most important passages of the whole Old
Testament. The "Suffering Servant" is Israel
portrayed in the guise of an individual. At the
beginning and end of the poem (verses 52:13-
15 and 53:10-12) God speaks, announcing
that his Servant will be highly exalted. In the
central portion (verses 53:1-9) the kings of
the nations speak. They come to see that the
meaning of Israel's tragedy was not merely
that the people had experienced the discipline
of divine judgment. That was part of it, but
there was a much deeper truth. Israel's suffering was *vicarious,* that is, it was borne for
others. Through the Servant's affliction, the
nations were made whole, restored to health,
"justified" or made right. This is the most
astounding truth of the Bible: that God
chooses the way of humiliation, suffering, rejection, and defeat to make known his victory

and sovereignty to the world. And this is the truth which is fulfilled and "made flesh" in the New Testament.

Questions to Think About

1. Is history purposeful or accidental in character? Compare modern interpretations of history, like Marxism and Progress, with the biblical sense of Providence.

2. In what sense is the return of the exiles comparable to the Exodus? Why does the Bible regard both events as "good news"?

3. What is Second Isaiah's understanding of the election or special choice of Israel? Compare Genesis 12:1-4. Do you find Second Isaiah's blending of the theme of God's universal sway and his particular choice of Israel to be a paradox?

4. Second Isaiah believed that God used Cyrus, even though the latter was unaware of it, for the accomplishment of his purpose. Could the same thing be said of modern political leaders? Is this the mean-

ing of Psalm 76:10—"Surely the wrath of man shall praise thee"?

5. How does Second Isaiah understand the meaning of suffering? In what sense is the Servant's sacrifice effective in removing guilt?

6. Even though Second Isaiah believed that *Israel* was to perform the role of the Suffering Servant, was the Christian Church justified in reading Isaiah 53 in the light of the Cross?

7. If the Church is the "New Israel," does it participate in the mission of the Suffering Servant?

Footnotes

1. The Unknown Prophet of the Exile is usually called the Second Isaiah to distinguish him from the earlier Isaiah of Jerusalem (740-700 B.C.) whose prophecies are found in the first section of the Book of Isaiah.

2. For an excellent exposition of some of these poems, see Paul Tillich, *The Shaking of the Foundations* (Charles Scribner's Sons, 1948), Chs. 2, 4, 12.

STUDY V:

The People of the Law

This study brings us to one of the most important, though for many Protestants the most difficult, phases of the biblical drama. The spotlight now falls on Ezra and Nehemiah, two men who played a decisive role in the formation of the community known as Judaism. It has been said that Israel went into exile as a nation and returned as a Church. The word "Judaism" refers to Israel which was no longer a national kingdom but a re-

---

STUDY PASSAGES

1. Nehemiah 9:6-38
2. Psalm 118
3. Psalm 1
4. Psalm 19:7-14
5. Psalm 119

---

ligious community. This worshiping community was an ellipse with two centers: the Temple and the Law.

The First Zionists

To see this in proper perspective, let's resume the story from the time of Second Isaiah, practically a century earlier than the period of Ezra. Shortly after Babylonia capitulated to the Persian armies, Cyrus of Persia issued an edict allowing Jews the privilege of returning to Palestine. So Jewish immigrants began their homeward trek to Zion (Jerusalem). When they arrived they found things in ruin. The Temple was destroyed, the walls of Jerusalem were leveled, the cities desolate. However, inspired by the prophecies of Haggai and Zechariah, they set about rebuilding the Temple, a project which was completed in 515 B.C.

Then Ezra came onto the scene, according to the sequence of events given by the historian who wrote the books of Ezra and Nehemiah. By permission of the Persian king, in the year 458 B.C. he led a caravan of Jews back to Palestine. Most important, he brought with him a copy of "the book of the law of Moses," and he lost no time in convening the Israelites to hear the reading of this lawbook. One of the solemn moments in Israel's history is described in Nehemiah 8—9, the occasion of the reading of the Law to the people, the offering of a prayer of penitence and gratitude, and the covenant pledge of the people "to walk in God's law, which was given by Moses the servant of God." On this occasion the people determined to learn from the lessons of history and, in the grace of God, to start all over. A few years later Nehemiah, a cupbearer to the Persian king, received permission to return to Palestine as Persian governor. After a memorable midnight tour around the city of Jerusalem, he organized the Jews for work and in a little less than two months the walls were rebuilt. So under the religious leadership of Ezra and the states-

manship of Nehemiah the "congregation of
Israel" took a new lease on life. It seemed as
if the glowing promises spoken by prophets
like Second Isaiah were on the verge of fulfillment (See RB, pp. 133-137.)

A Kingdom of Priests

The vitality of Judaism is indicated by the
great amount of biblical literature which
comes from this period. Indeed, the whole
Old Testament in its present form is stamped
indelibly with the influence of this religious
way of life. In this study, therefore, we can
do little more than scratch the surface of biblical Judaism. Our basic concern is to enter
into the life of this community out of which,
in the fullness of God's time, Christianity
emerged.

The best way to prepare for this study is to
familiarize yourself with the account of Ezra's
career as related in the following sequence of
chapters: Ezra 7–8; Nehemiah 8; Ezra 9–10;
Nehemiah 9–10. (The chapters should be

read in that order.) In these chapters you will find an emphasis upon ritual or "priestly" matters, and the concern for maintaining the purity of the faith by rigid laws against mixed marriages. Especially you should give attention to the account of Ezra's reading the Law (Nehemiah 8:1-8) and the prayer which followed shortly after (Nehemiah 9:6-38).

Notice that the prayer strikes a note which is characteristic of Israel's faith. It is a proclamation of "the mighty acts of the Lord" by which Israel had been brought onto the stage of history with a unique vocation. Penitently the people acknowledge that the Exile had come as God's judgment upon their unfaithfulness; gratefully they rejoice in the new Exodus from Babylonian captivity; solemnly they vow to manifest their faith and gratefulness by obeying the Law. This is one of the supreme confessions of faith to be found in the Old Testament.

The Stone That the Builders Rejected

Aside from this prayer, two psalms have been selected—one dealing with worship in the Jerusalem Temple (Psalm 118), and the other dealing with the place of the Law (Psalm 1).

Psalm 118 belongs in the setting of worship, for it is really a processional hymn which celebrates God's gracious acts in Israel's history. Imagine the scene: the procession forms for the ascent to "the Hill of the Lord"—the Temple. The choir is in the lead, and the throng of worshipers follow. After a call to worship by the choir leader (verses 1-4) the choir sings an anthem as the whole procession moves forward (verses 5-18). Then the Temple gates are thrown open (verses 19-20), and while the choir sings a climactic strain (verses 21-24), the choral procession surrounds the altar (verse 27). The whole congregation is united in this act of worship, so much so that the singular pronoun "I" is used throughout the psalm.

It has been suggested that this psalm may have been composed to celebrate a great event in the life of Israel after the Exile, perhaps Nehemiah's rebuilding of the walls of Jerusalem. In any case, the psalm voices the gratitude of a people who discerned the hand of God in their history, repeatedly delivering them from the strangle hold of enemies and giving them a place in the divine plan. The key passage is verses 21-24, especially the jubilant cry that the Stone which the builders had rejected has become the cornerstone of the foundation (compare Isaiah 28:16). The Stone is the remnant of Israel. Other builders would have rejected this stone as poor material, but God had been preparing in the furnace of suffering a "well-tested stone," with which he would carry forward his redemptive work in history.

Delight in God's Law

The first Psalm expresses the blessedness which comes from obeying God's Will. Re-

member that when the Israelite thought of
God's Law, he did not think of a Heavenly
Policeman who coldly enforces statutes;
rather, he thought of the God who had graciously redeemed Israel and had entered into
covenant with his people. In a previous unit
we noticed that from the very first the Covenant and the Law were linked together. As
time went on, many laws were added to the
covenant faith, and in Ezra's time, or shortly
after, the Law was identified especially with
the first five books of the Old Testament, the
so-called Five Books of Moses. You would
think that obeying the many laws of this Law
would be burdensome. But reading the first
Psalm will disclose that Judaism took an entirely different attitude, for the chief concern
was that of glorifying God in all daily actions.
(See also Psalm 19:7-14 and Psalm 119.)

Ezra's great reform had its strengths, but it
also had dangers which were evident to those
who were nurtured in the prophetic heritage.
(See RB, pp. 137–143.) It is one thing to de-

light in God's Will; it is another to be so self-righteously sure of what God's Will is in specific situations that men thank God that they are not as other people. Perhaps our churches fall into this danger in so far as a middle-class code of "thou shalts" and "thou shalt nots" is proclaimed as the standard of goodness; and leaders who claim that America's foreign policy is based on the Sermon on the Mount imply self-righteously that our enemies are the real sinners who fall short of the glory of God. According to the prophets, God's Will brought his people under judgment; God had a controversy with Israel. If you think seriously about how difficult it is to gain approval before God on the basis of our moral goodness, maybe you can anticipate why the Christian Gospel protests against all "legalism" and "moralism" and puts man's relation with God on an entirely different basis from the Law.[1]

Questions to Think About

1. Israel's prophets had affirmed that God reveals himself in events of history; Judaism tended to believe that God's revelation is given in the Book of the Law. Do you see any difference in these two positions?

2. Compare what the words "obey the law of God" would mean to a prophet like Jeremiah and a priest like Ezra.

3. The first Psalm suggests that if one obeys the Will of God he will enjoy security, influence, and long life. Do you think this should be the basis for obeying God? If not, what should it be?

4. It is said that in the state of Israel today there is no higher court of appeal, for the decisions of the rabbinical court are considered to be the very "decisions of God." Is the Will of God for specific situations so clearly definable?

5. In Acts 4:8-12 Peter applied the passage concerning the Rejected Stone to Jesus,

the foundation of God's New Building—
the Church. Is this the deeper meaning of
the passage?

6. Despite constant hardship and persecu-
tion, from the time of the oppression in
Egypt to the Nazi ovens at Buchenwald,
the Jewish people have survived, whereas
other nations have disappeared. How
should a Christian view the miracle of
"the eternal survival of the Jew"?

7. Does one gain the status of God's approval by obeying God's laws? Turn to
Psalm 130. How does a Christian look
upon Jewish "legalism"? upon current
"moralism"?

Footnote

1. See Paul's discussion of "justification by
faith" and not by "works of the law" in Romans
1–8. Also see RB, pp. 226–233.

Victory Through Defeat

The historical drama, of which God is the
protagonist, has now reached its climax. The
New Testament opens with the exuberant
claim that God's promises made by the prophets are being fulfilled (see RB, pp. 153-157,
165-179). John the Baptist, the last of the
Hebrew prophets before the Messianic Age,
appears on the scene proclaiming that the
Day of Judgment is at hand. Jesus steps onto
the stage of history at that time of crisis, and
his message is pitched to a key of urgency:
"The time is fulfilled, and the kingdom of God

STUDY PASSAGES

1. Acts 10:34-43
2. Mark 8:27 to 9:13
3. I Corinthians 1:17 to 2:9

---

is at hand; repent, and believe in the gospel"
(Mark 1:14).

The Christ Event

In Study IV it was pointed out that the Christian word "gospel" has its scriptural background in passages of Second Isaiah where
the prophet, like a herald, announces the
Good News of the coming of God's redemption. Likewise in the New Testament the Gospel is the Good News of God's Redemptive
Rule (Kingdom). The Good News centers in
what *God does,* his action for the renewal and
re-creation of human life. Moreover, the New
Testament proclaims that the Good News is
Jesus himself, his words and works which
confront men with the authority of one who
is uniquely *anointed* as God's agent (this is the
meaning of "Messiah," or "Christ"). And
above all, the Gospel focuses on the Crucifixion, and the other side of this event, the
Resurrection. If the Exodus was a mighty act
of God, if the deliverance of Jewish exiles

from captivity was a divine deed, then God's greatest miracle in history was what John Knox calls "the Christ Event"—the whole life, death, and resurrection of Jesus, together with the emergence of the Church.[1]

The written Gospels (Matthew, Mark, Luke, John) are not "biographies" in our sense of the word, so much as they are confessions of faith, written out of the intense conviction that in the man Jesus, God had performed a great work of redemption. This does not mean that the Gospels belong in the category of fiction or fantasy, for the gospel story is based securely upon the earthly career of a historical person. Nevertheless, Jesus' words and works were remembered in the experience of those who, after the Crucifixion and Resurrection, were convinced that he was God's Messiah. In the earliest Gospel (Mark), for instance, the whole focus of interest is the Passion of Christ. An even earlier formulation of the Christian gospel is found in Peter's sermon as recorded in Acts 10:34-

43—a passage which you should take time out to read, for it could be called the Gospel of Mark in miniature. (On the "life of Jesus," see further RB, pp. 157-165, 183-203.)

The Denouement of the Historical Drama

To appreciate the Christian claim that the Christ Event is the fulfillment and climax of the previous episodes of the biblical drama, let's take a brief glance backward. The biblical drama begins by describing in pictorial terms men's estrangement from God, from each other, and from their own true selfhood. To deal with this general human predicament God took the initiative—so we are told in Genesis 12:1-4—and called Abraham, promising him that his descendants would be a blessing to all nations. So Israel was called and formed as a community in order that this people might be the instrument for the accomplishment of God's plan in history. But Israel's record was one of persistent defiance of the covenant loyalty, and the fall of the

nation was interpreted by prophets as the discipline of God's judgment. Then a fresh start
was made after the Exile, but Israel became
so engrossed in saving her life by strict obedi-
ence to the Law that the world mission described by Second Isaiah was lost to sight
(see the Book of Jonah). At last "in the ful-
ness of time" came Jesus of Nazareth.

Then came, at a predetermined moment, a moment
in time and of time,
A moment not out of time, but in time, in what
we call history: transecting, bisecting, the
world of time, a moment in time but not like
a moment of time,
A moment in time but time was made through that
moment: for without the meaning there is no
time, and that moment of time gave the meaning.[2]

So the Christian faith affirms that in this "moment of time," which divides history into B.C.
and A.D., God has made a new beginning, has
introduced the New Age. Through Christ
men were brought into a new relation with
God, and as a corollary into a new relation
with one another. Jeremiah's prophecy of the

New Covenant had been fulfilled! (See Study III.) When the shadow of the Cross fell upon the table at the Last Supper, Jesus said to his disciples: "This cup is the new covenant in my blood" (Luke 22:20).

Who Do You Say That I Am?

Within this context of the fulfillment of God's promises made by the prophets we can discuss the story of Peter's confession at Caesarea-Philippi (Mark 8:27 ff.). Since this is the turning point in Mark's Passion story, your best preparation would be to read the whole Gospel through. The recurring question is: Who is this Stranger who speaks with authority, who performs mighty acts, who is rejected by the religious authorities and misunderstood by his own disciples, and who finally goes his lonely way to the Cross? Jesus himself is the question mark. "Who do *you* say that I am?" All thought and action is dependent upon the answer one gives to the question of the identity of Jesus. Neutrality is out of the question for any of us.

Notice that the mystery was heightened for the disciples, right after they recognized Jesus' messianic identity, by his announcement that his vocation was that of the Suffering Servant and that those who follow after him must share his suffering. Why was the Cross *necessary* in the accomplishment of God's purpose? It was generally believed that the Messiah would come to restore the lost fortunes of the Israelite nation and achieve thereby a victory which would be clear to all. How incredible that Isaiah 53, which Second Isaiah had applied to the sufferings of Israel (see Study IV), could be a description of the role of the triumphant Messiah! Mark here affirms the Christian gospel: that the suffering-and-death of the Christ is God's mighty act of deliverance.

The story of the Transfiguration (Mark 9:2-13) connects the Crucifixion-Resurrection with the previous episodes of the biblical drama. In the disciples' vision Moses (the Lawgiver) and Elijah (Israel's prophet *par excellence*) appear in company with Jesus, symbolizing the truth that in Christ, Israel's whole past has become luminous with meaning. The New Covenant is the fulfillment of the Old. In a kind of religious ecstasy the disciples perceive the splendid uniqueness of Jesus, but the sequel of Mark's story shows how they could not really understand the divine victory which lay on the other side of the Cross. Their continuing lack of faith is a commentary on Jesus' rebuke in Mark 9:33.

The Scandal of the Cross

The theme of the mystery of the Cross is treated at greater length in a letter which Paul addressed to the church at the Greek city of Corinth (I Corinthians 1:17–2:9). Here Paul points out that to the non-Christian the Cross is either "foolishness" or a "stumbling block." If Christianity were only the preaching of a loftier ethic or the belief in one God or even "the Fatherhood of God and the brotherhood of man" the world would have little difficulty with this faith. But the trouble is that Christianity proclaims the wisdom of God in what men consider foolishness, and the power of God in what men consider weakness and defeat. Take away the Cross, says Paul, and there is no gospel to proclaim. The Cross is the distinctive Christian symbol of God's victory in apparent defeat. "By this sign conquer."

Some of you may think it strange that we do not focus our attention first on Jesus' teachings as found in the Sermon on the Mount (see RB, pp. 229-233). The reason for this is that early Christians did not start there. They started, rather, with a recital of the story of Christ's Passion and the proclamation of his Resurrection. Teachings and ethical exhortations had their proper place *after* converts were made. As D. T. Niles observes: "The Sermon on the Mount is more a statement of what will happen to a man when he allows Jesus to get hold of him, than a statement of what a man must do if he is to follow

Jesus."[3] The Good News was not an ethical code or a new religious belief. It was, rather, the proclamation that God had actively confronted men in history in the man Jesus, and the evidence of this was that God had raised Jesus from the dead and called into existence a New Community. "God was in Christ," overcoming the sin which finds expression in our separation from God, from each other, and from our true selves, and restoring men to the unity and peace which God intends for his creation.

Questions to Think About

1. Why is the Cross a "scandal," that is, a stumbling block, to the non-Christian? Are you familiar with this "scandalous" Christianity or a more watered-down version?
2. What is the difference between "the wisdom of the world" and the "hidden wisdom of God"? Does the latter provide any information which could be acquired otherwise by hard study? Or is it a matter

of basic presuppositions which underlie intellectual activity?

3. Is there any real significance in the fact that the appearance of Jesus Christ has divided our Western calendar into B.C. and A.D.? What has the death of a Jewish carpenter hundreds of years ago got to do with your life today?

4. Why *must* the Messiah suffer? What view of man's problem and God's answer are here presupposed? Why is Jesus' death different from the martyrdom of Socrates, Lincoln, or Gandhi?

5. Traditional Christianity has affirmed that Jesus is the "God-Man." What is the experience which underlies this creedal statement? Is the paradox necessary? (See RB, pp. 203-207.)

6. What is wrong with saying that the essence of Christianity is the Golden Rule or the Sermon on the Mount?

7. Toynbee says that the Transfiguration is the key to the Christian interpretation of

history. (See C. H. Dodd's summary in *The Bible Today*, pp. 126-129.) Does Christ really disclose the hidden meaning of history? If so, what difference does this make?

Footnotes

1. See John Knox, *On the Meaning of Christ* (Charles Scribner's Sons, 1947).

2. T. S. Eliot, from Choruses from *The Rock*, VII, *Collected Poems 1909-1935* (Harcourt, Brace and Co., 1936), p. 199. Used by permission.

3. *That They May Have Life* (Harper & Brothers, 1951), p. 47. This is one of the finest books on the Christian Gospel.

The Church and the World

In this study our attention focuses on a "new emergent" in history: the Church of Jesus Christ. From the very first, Christianity was anything but individualism. Indeed John Knox insists that the phrase "individual Christian" is a contradiction in terms, for the very word "Christian" implies a social reality, a community. Christianity is an *esprit de corps.* Jesus himself conceived his mission to be that of calling a Remnant of Israel—twelve disciples, corresponding to the twelve tribes of Israel. And when the meaning of Jesus'

STUDY PASSAGES

1. I Peter 2:4-10
2. Ephesians 2:11-22
3. Matthew 28:16-20

life, death, and resurrection came upon these
disciples with overwhelming power at Pente-
cost (Acts 2), a great miracle occurred. This
small community became a dynamic and mili-
tant Church, with a message which "turned
the world upside down" and a gospel which
was carried enthusiastically to the ends of the
earth. The Acts of the Apostles gives the
story of the emerging, expanding Church.
And every line of the New Testament pre-
supposes the New Community.

The Israel of God

While stressing the newness of the Church
we must also keep in mind the relation of this
community to the whole Old Testament de-
velopment. The Old Testament affirms that
God chose and formed a People to be the instrument of his saving work in history. Israel
was not just a race or a nation; Israel was
God's *creation* (Isaiah 43:15; 44:2). Having
raised Israel from the miserable lot of slavery
in Egypt, God entered into covenant with his

people and through the long years that followed, educated and disciplined them in order that they might understand more deeply the meaning of their sacred calling. It was Second Isaiah who understood most clearly Israel's God-given role. Israel was to be a "light to the Gentiles" and a Servant whose sufferings would benefit all mankind. However, in the period of Judaism the people lost sight of their missionary calling. Their devotion to the Law sharpened the barrier between Jew and non-Jew, and even separated them from their near relatives, the Samaritans. The last two centuries before Christ witnessed a resurgence of Jewish nationalism which led in time to the Jewish war against Rome. In A.D. 70 the Romans destroyed the Temple, leveled Jerusalem, and removed the last vestiges of Jewish statehood.

So in the fullness of time God acted once again to form a community, no longer bound by the restrictions of Judaism but open to all men—whether Jew or Gentile—on the basis of faith. The Church is the New Israel, the community of the New Covenant, "God's own People." In this study we shall come to terms with the nature of this community and its mission to the world.

God's New Creation

Of the many passages in the New Testament which deal with this subject three have been selected for study. You will find that each passage deals with an important characteristic of the Church. The first of these (I Peter 2:4-10) brings down the accent upon the truth that this Community has been established by God's action through Christ, the "living Stone" who is the foundation of a "spiritual House." The Church is not a social organization or a human institution which can be understood by sociological analysis; it is, rather, a creation of God who has chosen the "rejected Stone" (Jesus Christ) as the foundation. Of course, this harks back to our previous discussion of Psalm 118 and the prophetic doctrine of the Remnant of Israel which God preserved for the accomplishment of his purpose in history. Notice that the expressions in verse 9 previously had been applied to the chosen people at the time of the making of the Covenant (compare Exodus 19:4-6); now they are applied to the New Israel.

A Fellowship of Love

The second passage (Ephesians 2:11-22) stresses the unity of the Church which has been redeemed by Christ's sacrifice. Here you will want to look into the biblical meaning of the word "peace." We usually think of peace as the absence of war; but in the Bible peace has a more positive meaning. Peace is a state of harmony, wholeness, and welfare within the community. And it is a basic biblical premise that there cannot be right relations within the community unless man is in right relation with God, for separated from God men are at odds with themselves and with one another. Only as men stand in mutual relation to the Center, God, can there be true peace, true community. As Old Testament prophets looked away from the broken and fractured society of Israel, they anticipated the coming of the age of the Messiah when the barriers of separation would be overcome and men would be brought into a new relation with God and with one another. The New Testament affirms that the Messianic Age has dawned, and that this peace is already a reality within the Church. Through the power of Christ's sacrifice, the walls of hostility are removed, broken relationships are healed, and men receive anew their lost humanity. The Church is a fellowship of love —the highest endowment of God's Spirit (see I Corinthians 13; I John 4:7-12).

Go into All the World

The last passage (Matthew 28:16-20) is a brief statement of the mission of the Church to the world. The Church is a community set apart from the world—"elect from every nation, yet one o'er all the earth," as the well-known hymn says. Indeed, the New Testament word for church (*ecclesia*) literally means "called out," and appropriately suggests the basic conception of God in Christ calling men out of the world into a unique fellowship. Nevertheless, the Church is not a parasite on the world; it is more like an army of white corpuscles in the blood stream of humanity. The Church has inherited the mission of the Servant described by Second Isaiah: to be a light to the nations and to carry the Good News to the ends of the earth. Its task is to bear witness to God's Kingdom, which has already been manifested in Jesus Christ, but which cannot come in its fullness until all the kingdoms of the world have been incorporated into the empire of Christ. The Church, by virtue of the commission from her Lord, must be socially responsible, missionary minded, and world redeeming.

T. S. Eliot has written some lines which

are reminiscent of a famous passage in Matthew (16:18) and which express the relation between the Church and the World:

There shall always be the Church and the World,
And the heart of man
Shivering and fluttering between them choosing and
 chosen,
Valiant, ignoble, dark, and full of light
Swinging between hell gate and heaven gate
And the gates of hell shall not prevail.[1]

Questions to Think About

1. In the light of the whole biblical drama, is it more accurate to say that Jesus founded the Church or that he re-created the already existing Church?

2. What is the relation between the Church and the many "churches" which we know in this country? Does the real unity of the Church lie in organization? If not, what is the basis of its unity?

3. What is the essential difference between Old Israel and "New Israel"? Does this

difference suggest why the Christian church is, in principle, a universal rather than an ethnic community?

4. "The Church is not a human institution but a creation of God." What does this mean? Why cannot the Church be understood from the standpoint of social science?

5. What does it mean to say that the Age of the Messiah has already arrived? Has the angelic promise, "peace on earth," already been experienced within the Church, even though the world does not have peace?

6. Why cannot the Christian be satisfied with the popular view that there is truth in all religions and that missionaries should stay home?

7. Does the difficulty of ethical decision arise from the fact that the Christian is both a member of the church and a citizen of the world? Should the Christian

be antiworldly, that is, negative toward "secular" issues?

Footnote

1. T. S. Eliot, *The Rock* (Harcourt, Brace and Co., 1934). Used by permission.

STUDY VIII:

History's Finale

Like any drama, the biblical drama moves from beginning to end. This elementary observation is exceedingly important for the understanding of the biblical view of history. Unlike ancient Greek historians who believed that history spins in circles like a ferris wheel, or unlike some modern historians who believe that the historical process is a phase of the growth and decay of nature, the Bible affirms that the historical drama moves in the direction of a goal. "Time marches on." However, it is not the time of

---

STUDY PASSAGES
1. Revelation 21:1-7
2. Revelation 21:22 to 22:5
3. I Corinthians 15:12-28 and 51-58

---

nature which is measured by the cycle of the seasons; it is, rather, the Time of God's purpose.

The Horizons of History

It has been observed that when it comes to the interpretation of history there are three possible views: (1) History is meaningless flux from which the religious man seeks escape (Hinduism, Buddhism); (2) history secretes its own meaning in the course of cultural evolution (Progress, Marxism); and (3) the meaning of history is *revealed* by God who, as Creator, transcends the whole finite world of sense experience. The biblical view is that the meaning of history has its source in the God who assigns the beginning and the end, and who surveys and participates in the drama in its entirety.

In the first study unit we considered the "prologue" to the biblical drama of God's action in history; now we turn our attention to the "epilogue." It should be obvious that we cannot speak of either the "first things" or the "last things" except in the language of religious symbolism. In both cases we are dealing with ultimates which lie beyond the range of our finite knowledge. Therefore we must speak in the language of faith—faith which rests not upon our ability to fathom or chart the beginning and the end, but upon the meaning which has been revealed in that unique series of historical events beginning with the Exodus and culminating in the Christ Event. It is the Christian faith that human history as we know it is bounded by Beginning and End—two horizons which recede into God's Eternity. (See RB, pp. 254-264.)

Paradise Regained

A good place to begin the discussion is the description of the New Heaven and New Earth found in the last book of the New Testament. This is an exceedingly difficult book to understand because it is written in a symbolic code which cannot be deciphered easily. Much damage has been done by people who have read this book as though they were gazing into a crystal ball. We have tried to facilitate the study by selecting two brief passages (21:1-7 and 21:22 to 22:5) in which the symbolism is not quite so obtuse. Even so, there are references which will not mean much unless you check with a good commentary (see the *Westminster Study Edition of the Holy Bible*). For instance, "the Sea was no more" (21:1) is a mythological allusion to the Great Deep, the symbol of rebellious powers which God has held in check. In other words, this is not just the drying up of water, but the overcoming of hostile powers arrayed against God's rule. And the Lamb, of course, is the triumphant Christ (see John 1:29).

Two things are especially noteworthy in these passages. First, the description of the New Heaven and New Earth gathers up **some** of the symbols of the Garden of Eden (see "the Tree of Life"). Thus the end of the drama is related to the beginning, the New Creation to the First Creation. In the second place, observe that the consummation of history is symbolized under the figure of the New Jerusalem descending from the skies— the City of God. In previous studies we have found that Jerusalem in the Bible is more than a city, as we ordinarily think of it. To the Israelite, Jerusalem meant much more than Athens to the ancient Greek or Washington to the American. Jerusalem was the symbol of God's Rule among men and the working out of his redemptive purpose spanning across history from the Exodus to the Messianic Age. Medieval maps which pinpointed Jerusalem as the center of the universe were based on bad geography and astronomy, but they expressed a profound religious truth. Jerusalem, to the man of faith, stands for *meaning* which is the very foundation of Israel and the Church. Here, then, we find the bold claim that history will ultimately fulfill and complete this meaning, and that all nations will find their peace and unity by walking in the light of the New Jerusalem (21:24-26; compare Isaiah 2:14).

Thus the Bible begins with a vision of Paradise Lost and concludes with a vision of the coming of God's Kingdom. In between this prologue and epilogue unfolds the drama of God's entrance into the human struggle to win back his lost creation and to restore man to the peace, unity, and blessedness which he intends for mankind. God's strategy includes the choice and discipline of a People, and finally the way of the Cross; but the end of his redemptive activity is the final conquest of sin, death, and all powers which corrupt and threaten history. The Church lives by this hope, and prays and strives for the coming of God's Kingdom.

The Decisive Battle Is Won!

This brings us to the third passage, a portion of I Corinthians 15. The background of this passage is the Hebraic view of the Last Judgment when the dead will be "raised up" in order that the faithful may share in the final conclusion of the historical drama.[1] In much of the chapter Paul argues that the "body" that will be raised is not the physical body, but a *spiritual body* which cannot be visualized. It is worth noting, in passing, that the body is the symbol of the *person* in the wholeness of his personality, the unique self who finds life in relation to other persons. Rather than stumbling over details, we should realize that what Paul is saying is this: the individual is *given* a future by God, though exactly how, says Paul, is "a mystery." However, the important point to notice in this passage is that God's victory over sin and death has already occurred—even before the End which is described in Revelation as the New Heaven and New Earth. Of this the Christian has already been given the assurance in the Resurrection of Christ. For his victory is the "first fruits" which gives promise that the harvest is coming. Or, as Paul puts it elsewhere, through Christ men have been given the Holy Spirit as the "earnest" or *guarantee* of what is to come (II Corinthians 1:22, 5:5). (See RB, pp. 208-226, 264-267.)

This is only to say that the center of gravity in the Christian faith is not a longing for a Consummation which has not been realized. The distinctive note of Christianity is that the Messiah has already come, that he has already won the victory, and that through him men may now taste the life of the Kingdom. To those who respond to the Christ-Event in faith is given the hope that ultimately God's Kingdom will come in fullness and glory, and that "God will be everything to everyone." Oscar Cullmann has put the matter in an apt figure of speech. In a war the decisive battle often occurs in an early stage of the campaign, and though the fighting continues until the end of the war, the issue already has been decided. So for the

Christian the decisive battle has been won by Christ, and to the Church is given the "guarantee" that the struggle of history will end with God's "V-Day"—the Kingdom of God.[2] As D. T. Niles puts it: "The Gospel is a call to a battle whose final victory is already won."[3]

Questions to Think About

1. What does the Bible mean by the phrase "the Kingdom of God"? (See RB, p. 187.)
2. In what sense has the Kingdom already been realized through the life, death, and resurrection of Jesus Christ and the creation of the Church? In what sense is the Kingdom still to come?
3. What is wrong with identifying the Kingdom with the "better world" which men hope to achieve, either through progressive effort or revolutionary fiat?
4. If it is wrong to speak of "building the Kingdom on earth," in what sense are men "co-workers with God"?

5. How does the Christian's "ultimate hope" affect his social and political responsibilities in the present historical order? What are some of the "proximate hopes" which we may expect to realize in history?

6. Traditional Christianity has preferred to express belief in the future life in terms of the resurrection of the body, rather than the dualistic Greek doctrine of the immortality of the soul. Why is the former more adequate?

7. What does it mean to say that Christ has already won the decisive victory over sin, death, and the powers of darkness?

Footnotes

1. For an interpretation of the words of the Apostles' Creed "I believe in the resurrection of the body," see Reinhold Niebuhr, *Beyond Tragedy* (Charles Scribner's Sons, 1938).

2. See Oscar Cullmann, *Christ and Time* (Westminster Press, 1950), especially Ch. 5.

3. D. T. Niles, *That They May Have Life* (Harper & Brothers, 1951), p. 21.

Suggestions for
Bible Study Leaders

Purpose

Those who plan to set up a Bible Study Group should have at the outset some understanding of the uniqueness of the venture. This is not a literary circle devoted to the study of one of the "great books." The uniqueness of a Bible Study Group lies in that which is at the center: the Bible. The Bible continues to exert a strange power over men's lives because it searchingly exposes the nature of the human predicament and witnesses to the decisive answer. Man's question and God's answer: this is the central concern of the Bible. Since all of us are inescapably involved in human existence, with its glory and complexity and tragedy, there should be a place in the group for any concerned person. Those with Christian convictions (and probably they will be in the majority) will find in the Bible a deeper understanding of the relevance of the Christian faith to the issues of personal life and history. The skeptic who is sincerely seeking for light on the meaning of human existence may discover that the Bible "'speaks to his condition." But all members of the group will have a common purpose: to hear what the Bible says to us in our life-situation today.

The key word for Bible Study is *encounter*. What takes place in the group is personal encounter—with one another and with God who speaks to us through the Bible. This distinguishes Bible Study from the kind of classroom study in which our primary relation is to facts rather than persons. However, the personal encounter of a Bible Study Group is not that of a glorified "bull session" in which discussion is carried on in an argumentative spirit, usually without any common frame of reference. In this case the conversation has a common center, a common frame of reference. There will be disagreements, for we approach the Bible out of our private and cultural background, which usually means with a great deal of ignorance and even rebellion. However, it is the testimony of the ages that God speaks to us as persons when we enter into conversation with the Bible receptively, expectantly, honestly. Often this means that the presuppositions of the questions we bring to the Bible are challenged; often it means the realization that we have not asked the basic question; often it means being disturbed and changed at the very center of our being. But this is what we must expect if we risk an encounter with God.

Leadership

a) *Who should be the leader?* This is a difficult question. Some groups have effectively used the principle of rotation, that is, each time a different student member of the group is responsible for the meeting. Often this runs against the snag that some of the members are not yet far enough along in their understanding of the Bible; and if the blind lead the blind, probably everyone will fall into the ditch! Other groups have found that it is better to rely on a leader who is more mature in biblical understanding (this may be an advanced student in some cases, or a staff leader, a professor, a minister). No rule of thumb can be given, since groups vary so much and the Bible Study movement is still in an experimental stage in America.

b) Qualities of good leadership. The main task of the leader is to help the group to go to the heart of the biblical passage, so that there may be a genuine encounter with the Bible rather than a mere rearranging of prejudices. This means that the leader should have some ability in group discussion and should have a fairly good knowledge about the Bible (though not necessarily that of an "expert"). The good leader is the one who brings the discussion back to the biblical passage when it wanders astray, who patiently guides the discussion so that disagreements are fruitful, who encourages others to participate in the conversation, and who helps the group to go deeper than either pat answers or hasty rejection of what some may think they have outgrown. Above all, the leader is the "servant" of the group and should encourage the rest to have a sense of responsibility for the preparation and participation which will make the study a vital group experience.

c) *Preparation.* It cannot be emphasized too strongly that this is a *study* group in the best sense of the word. Therefore the success of the group depends on disciplined and serious preparation on the part of all members. At the minimum, this preparation must be the careful reading and prayerful pondering of the biblical passage with the aid of the Study Guide. This applies especially to the leader. His careful study of the material will enable him to discern what is central and what is peripheral in the group discussion. Also, he should be acquainted with the necessary background material for understanding the passage, turning whenever possible to a good commentary (see Bibliography).

d) Resource persons. Usually study groups include a "resource person" (a minister, teacher, staff member) who can be consulted when information is needed on a particular question. It is important to find the kind of person who is both congenial to students and who will not "lord it over the group" with his contributions. Frequently, however, adults tend to lean over backward on this matter, that is, they are so afraid of dominating the discussion that they do not speak until spoken to. Somehow this matter should be worked out so that the adult is actually a member of the group—on a level of equality with other participants rather than being set up on a pedestal because of his superior knowledge. Perhaps it would be well to forget about the conception of a "resource person," and think rather of team leadership, that is, a student and an adult who co-operate in preparing for the meeting and guiding the discussion so that it may be fruitful.

Procedure

First of all, help the members of the group to feel at home with each other. In a classroom you can get by without knowing who is sitting next to you, for your concern is with a body of factual knowledge, not a relation between persons. However, Bible Study—as we have said—is a relation with persons by means of the spoken word, and an encounter with God who comes to men personally through his Word. Since God's Truth comes to men personally, rather than as a body of "facts," we need the rapport of personal relationship in the group.

At some point in these informal proceedings the leader should open the discussion of the selected biblical passage. In some situations it would be well to have a brief prayer or a few moments of silence. As Alan Richardson observes, the important thing is that the entire Bible Study be carried on in an atmosphere of prayer.

The leader may begin by giving whatever background is necessary for the study of the passage. Perhaps on other days he could ask other members of the group to do this in order that the group as a whole may sense a shared responsibility. Above all, this principle of biblical interpretation should be followed in the group discussion:

(a) The first task is to discover what the biblical writer intended to say. This may involve such questions as: Who was the author? When did he write? What was the historical and cultural setting? To whom did he write? What message was he attempting to convey in the symbolism of language?

(b) Having established this as far as possible, then deal with the question as to what the passage says to *us* in our historical and cultural situation. Remember that "the letter killeth; it is the Spirit that giveth Life." The Bible should not be treated as a soothsayer's manual which gives us literal, specific directives on everything under the sun. As John Casteel has said, there are some places in the Bible where God does not say anything to us except, perhaps, "go read a commentary."

After a brief introduction of the historical setting of the passage, or perhaps before if you choose, it would be well to ask the group to read through the passage—or some portion of it—silently. Or you may decide to ask someone to read the passage, or a small unit of it, aloud. If there are difficult words, they should be explained. Perhaps light from another translation should be sought.

Sometimes groups have found it helpful to begin the discussion by attempting to paraphrase the passage in modern language, that is, "put it in your own words." This is a good discipline, for it demands (1) coming to terms with what the original writer meant to say, and (2) attempting to translate that meaning into our own categories. This may occasion the *interaction* between the world of the Bible and our world, which is the very essence of Bible conversation. Moreover, this gets away from the false idea of "private interpretation" of the Bible. We do not have the right to make the Bible say what we think it ought to say. First we must discover what the original writer was saying to his time, and then seek to translate that meaning into the parallel situations of our time. Group conversation around the Bible, guided by the Holy Spirit, will lead to a deeper understanding of biblical Truth. Don't be afraid to raise the "unorthodox" questions, for these may help to sharpen the issues, and God may use the skeptic to lead us into new truth. On the other hand, don't be afraid of "orthodoxy"

—only try to "beat the crust back into the batter" of Christian experience. The questions included in the Study Guide at the end of each unit may help to focus the discussion.

The discussion should move according to blocks of Scripture which the leader has isolated in his private preparation. When he senses that it is time to move on, he may give a summary of a given unit of material. Above all, the leader should not be anxious about the discussion, as though its success were dependent upon his keeping it going. Don't be troubled when there are periods of silence. Don't try to hurry the group forward because of the consideration that a given amount of material has to be covered; it is better to stay with a passage until you sense the group is ready to move on. Don't answer important questions impatiently; it may be better for the group to come to the answer for itself. As a leader, your purpose is not to lead the group to the conclusions which you foresaw during your preparation; rather, let the conclusion come out of the dialectic of the discussion.

Close on time if possible. The leader may signal the end of the discussion by giving a brief summary, and showing the relation of the discussion to the previous study session or to studies that follow. Normally the summary should be followed by a brief prayer, such as the prayer found in Psalm 139:23-24.

Keep in mind that the foregoing remarks are only suggestions. No plan should be superimposed inflexibly upon a Bible Study Group.

Selected Bibliography

BOOKS ON THE BIBLE

Anderson, B. W., *Rediscovering the Bible* (Haddam House: Association Press, 1951).

——, *Understanding the Old Testament* (Prentice-Hall, 1957); Howard C. Kee and Franklin W. Young, *Understanding the New Testament* (Prentice-Hall, 1957). These companion volumes, written in nontechnical language, provide an introduction to the Bible for the general reader.

Dodd, C. H., *The Bible Today* (Macmillan, 1947). This superb book by a great scholar is just the thing for those who want an introduction to the whole Bible.

Herberg, Will, "Biblical Faith as *Heilgeschichte*: The Meaning of Redemptive History in Human Existence," *The Christian Scholar*, Vol. 39 (March, 1956), pp. 25-31.

Miller, Alexander, *The Renewal of Man* (Doubleday, 1955). Addressed to the questioning modern mind, this book spells out in contemporary terms the meaning of biblical faith.

Minear, Paul S., *Eyes of Faith* (Westminster, 1946). More difficult reading, but an incisive exposition of the biblical perspective.

Richardson, Alan, *A Preface to Bible Study* (Westminster, 1944). This little book, by an outstanding theologian who has been a leader in the British SCM, is excellent for our purpose.

Tillich, Paul, *The Shaking of the Foundations* (Scribner, 1948). These sermons, based on biblical passages, disclose the profound relevance of the Bible to man's situation today.

COMMENTARIES

Westminster Study Edition of the Holy Bible (Westminster Press). Based on the King James Version, this gives a brief introduction to each book of the Bible and a concise commentary at the foot of each page.

Interpreter's Bible (Abingdon-Cokesbury). The general articles and the commentary of biblical books are excellent aids for those who want to understand the Bible thoroughly.

The Torch Commentaries (London: SCM Press). This excellent series is designed for the general reader, and takes into consideration both the results of biblical scholarship and the emphasis of biblical theology.

Harper's Annotated Bible Series (Harper). Based on the King James Version, these inexpensive pamphlets are very useful.

The Moffatt New Testament Commentaries (Harper). Readable, excellent aids to study, based on the Moffatt translation.

Theological Word Book of the Bible, edited by Alan Richardson (Macmillan). This is a useful volume to consult for the meaning of some key word in the Bible.

PAMPHLETS ON BIBLE STUDY

Anderson, Puxley, *et al.*, "A Bird's-Eye View of
the Bible," *The Intercollegian,* December, 1951.
Reprints available from the YMCA or YWCA,
10¢.

de Dietrich, Suzanne, *Discovering the Bible.*
Available from World Council of Christian
Education, 156 Fifth Ave., New York 10, N. Y.,
50¢ apiece, 38¢ in quantities of 20 or more.
Useful as a guide for group study, or for in-
dividual reading.

de Haller, Marie-Jeanne, *A Living Record* (Geneva:
World's Student Christian Federation, 1949).
Available from USCC, 156 Fifth Ave., New
York 10, N. Y., 75¢ apiece. This is another
synoptic treatment of the Bible as a unity.

Richardson, Alan, *How to Read the Bible* (Church
Army Press). This helpful guide can be secured
from the British SCM.

STUDY GUIDES ON PARTICULAR BOOKS OF THE BIBLE

The Victory That Overcomes the World, A Study
Guide in Five Parts to the First Epistle of John,
prepared by William Hamilton. Available from
the USCC for 20¢ apiece, 15¢ in quantities of
10 or more.

Christ Our Life, eight studies in John 13–17
(Kandy Series No. 1). Available from the
USCC for 15¢.

The Church in the Sayings of Our Lord, a series
of twelve studies (Kandy Series No. 2); also
available from the USCC for 15¢.

"I Am God, and Not Man," a USCC Bible Study Guide to the Book of Hosea, by William Hamilton, 50¢.

Citizens of God's Kingdom, a USCC Bible Study Guide to the Sermon on the Mount, by Roger Lincoln Shinn, 15¢.